Young Heroes

James Quadrino
Wildlife Protector

Q.L. Pearce

KIDHAVEN PRESS
An imprint of Thomson Gale, a part of The Thomson Corporation

Detroit • New York • San Francisco
New Haven, Conn. • Waterville, Maine • London

© 2007 Thomson Gale, a part of The Thomson Corporation.

Thomson and Star Logo and KidHaven Press are trademarks and Gale is a registered trademark used herein under license.

For more information, contact
KidHaven Press
27500 Drake Rd.
Farmington Hills, MI 48331-3535
Or you can visit our Internet site at http://www.gale.com

ALL RIGHTS RESERVED.
No part of this work covered by the copyright hereon may be reproduced or used in any form or by any means—graphic, electronic, or mechanical, including photocopying, recording, taping, Web distribution or information storage retrieval systems—without the written permission of the publisher.

Every effort has been made to trace the owners of copyrighted material.

LIBRARY OF CONGRESS CATALOGING-IN-PUBLICATION DATA

Pearce, Q.L. (Querida Lee)
James Quadrino, wildlife protector / by Q.L. Pearce.
   p. cm. — (Young heroes)
Includes bibliographical references and index.
   ISBN-13: 978-0-7377-3612-0 (hardcover : alk. paper)
   ISBN-10: 0-7377-3612-7 (hardcover : alk. paper)
1. Quadrino, James Andrew, 1991– 2. Conservationists—United States—Biography—Juvenile literature. 3. Birds—Conservation—United States—Juvenile literature. I. Title.
QH31.Q83P43 2007
333.95'416092--dc22
[B]
                                          2006018755

Printed in the United States of America

Contents

Chapter One:
The Boy Who Saves Birds 4

Chapter Two:
Problems and Solutions 12

Chapter Three:
Success in the Field 21

Chapter Four:
The Work Continues 30

Notes 40
Glossary 42
For Further Exploration 43
Index 46
Picture Credits 48
About the Author 48

Chapter One

The Boy Who Saves Birds

James Andrew Quadrino is fascinated by the natural world. He is always ready to do his part to protect and preserve it. In 2004, at the age of thirteen, he was presented with the President's Environmental Youth Award. James was honored for his important work with the birds of his hometown, Staten Island, New York.

When a fire in a nature preserve destroyed the nesting sites of many birds on the island, James came to the rescue by building nesting boxes. Today he continues to monitor the boxes and creates new ones to suit the needs of a dozen different **species** of birds. He also makes presentations to schools, park centers, and community groups. James hopes to encourage other people to enjoy watching birds in their natural habitats. His goal is to restore the natural balance of bird populations.

James Quadrino and his twin brother, Joseph, were born in Staten Island on August 11, 1991. James also has an older brother, John.

The Boy Who Saves Birds

His mother, Maria, is a homemaker. His father, James Sr., is an electrician. The family includes two lively dogs: Ronaldo, a standard schnauzer, and Terry, a smooth fox terrier. There is also a feathered member of the Quadrino family—a canary named Verdinho, which means "little green" in Portuguese.

In many ways James is a typical teen. His favorite snacks are pizza and bagels. He sometimes settles down in front of the television to watch a program such as *Mythbusters* or *Jeopardy*. James also finds plenty of time for sports. He joined the Monsignor Farrell High School wrestling team because he knew the sport developed both physical and mental strength. He works hard at practice six days a week. Another favorite sport is soccer. James plays forward on the high school team. On Sundays, soccer is a family activity—James and his brothers play on a team with their father.

James Quadrino (far right) poses with his family at a White House ceremony in 2004.

Besides playing sports, James enjoys tinkering with robotics. As a captain on his school robotics team, he builds robots that are matched against others in competitions. He explains, "Each year there is a different task and we build a different robot. We build and test it in school, where the principal gave us a workshop room."[1]

Despite his interest in robotics, James's favorite school subject has always been biology, because he loves to learn about living things. For this reason his library includes many books about animals and nature. Two of his favorites are *Where the Red Fern Grows* by Wilson Rawls and *Song of the Dodo* by David Quammen. "Ever since I can remember, I was extremely interested in birds and other animals," James says. "I have an **insatiable** appetite to learn more about animals. I am a very curious person, and reading books makes me feel closer to them."[2]

Family Camping Trips

In addition to reading about animals, James learns about them firsthand by spending time outdoors—bird-watching, canoeing, fishing, and camping. The entire family—dogs included—sometimes camps in the forests of upstate New York or Pennsylvania. On a typical camping trip, James wakes up early to listen to the birds before a day of backpacking with his dad and brothers. His mother stays in camp, James says, because she is "scared of bears!"[3]

James's interest in animals developed very early. As a young child he often went with his family to a popular bike path on the edge of the D&R Canal in nearby

James (left), his mother, and brothers enjoy a family camping trip.

New Jersey. One day while riding his bike, he turned and rode, fully clothed, into the canal to catch a turtle. "My parents and passersby thought I was crazy," he says. "I caught him, identified him as a juvenile snapping turtle, and set him free."[4]

James's experiences with animals have not been limited to the United States. Because his mother is from Brazil, the family has traveled there six times. On every journey James has had a chance to learn more about birds and their natural habitats. On one trip he approached a toucan to take a photograph. The large bird did not want to be bothered and scrambled after him, he says, "like a dog chasing a cat."[5] James thought it was funny and scary at the same time to have such an amazing creature charging after him. The encounter only heightened his interest in bird behavior.

An Island Home

James did not have to travel far from home to learn about the **avian** world, however. Nestled at the southwestern tip of New York City, Staten Island is an ideal location for someone who is interested in the environment. It is known for its many historical sites, parks, and wildlife preserves. It is also home to the famed Staten Island Zoo, where James volunteers his time in the petting zoo. In one day he might clean the barn or feed and clean goats, mini horses, sheep, deer, cows, or **alpacas**. "I also clean the ducks' pool. In the afternoon I help to feed and play with the otters,"[6] he says.

Besides the zoo, another of James's favorite outdoor sites is Mount Loretto Unique Area, a 194-acre (78.5 hectares) nature preserve. When his mother taught at a church summer camp there, he often joined the campers for a weekly nature walk. He observed owls and gathered bird feathers.

Because of his love for birds and other animals, James was dismayed to learn that as developers clear land for homes, businesses, and roads, natural habitats disappear. The development of new communities shrinks grasslands and wooded areas. On Staten Island

The Boy Who Saves Birds

Development was not the only threat to bird nesting sites on Staten Island, however. One night in March 2000, James heard the scream of fire engine sirens. A historic building at Mount Loretto was aflame. "We could see the fire from far away,"[7] he recalls. The huge

Development on New York's Staten Island threatened the habitat of the tree swallow (pictured) and other birds.

James holds a baby tree swallow that was born in one of his nesting boxes.

and elsewhere, this has led to the loss of natural tree cavities where birds such as American kestrels, barn owls, eastern bluebirds, and wood ducks build their nests. When James learned of this crisis he was worried for the birds. The balance of the local **ecosystem** could be in danger because birds help to control rodent and insect populations.

blaze also destroyed many of the natural cavities where the birds at Mount Loretto build their nests. The birds had already lost many sites on the island due to land development. James knew that if they were to survive, it was time for people to act.

James read library books about Staten Island bird populations. He searched the Internet for information about nesting habits, egg laying, predators of birds and their young, and the development of birds from egg to adult. He interviewed local people who knew the park well and visited the Cornell University Laboratory of **Ornithology** in Ithaca, New York. Through his research, James learned that one solution was to provide the birds with nesting boxes that were similar in size and shape to natural tree cavities. These boxes would shelter the birds and keep their babies safe from **predators**. With his parents' help, James purchased supplies with which to build the boxes and began his project to help the cavity-nesting birds of Staten Island.

Chapter Two

Problems and Solutions

James's first step was to write to the New York State Department of Environment Conservancy (DEC) and explain his project. He met with officials from the group, who gave him permission for the project and helped him plan it. It would require a great deal of hard work, but James was not concerned. He felt confident because the staff of the DEC had faith in him. Soon his plan was underway.

Installing the nest boxes would not be the end of the project. James would have to monitor them, so he chose a site close to home. Mount Loretto was the best candidate for many reasons. It includes five different ecosystems that attract a wide variety of birds: marine/coastal, grassland, forest, and tidal and freshwater wetlands. Ancient beech trees, some as many as 230 years old, grow in certain areas. Other parts of the forest include old-growth white oak, black gum, swamp white oak, black birch, and red maple trees. This variety of trees

Problems and Solutions

had been a factor in the development of a diverse population of cavity-nesting birds. James carefully observed the birds that he expected to attract to learn about their preferred habitat, particularly the nesting sites they chose.

James made a short list of birds that populated the area during the breeding season. With his research to guide him, he identified possible sites for the nest boxes. Placing them along the edge of a wooded forest might attract house wrens, black-capped chickadees, and tufted titmice. Boxes in open fields might attract

With his father's help, James built these nesting boxes for the birds in a nearby nature reserve.

James holds an American kestrel, one of many types of birds that found shelter in the nesting boxes.

bluebirds, tree swallows, or American kestrels. "I decided to have bird boxes for bluebirds, American kestrels, barn owls, and wood ducks due to the habitat and birds' biology,"[8] James explains.

Getting to Work

Once he had selected the sites, James planned and built the sturdy boxes of untreated pine, cedar, or fir. To pro-

Problems and Solutions

tect the birds from the environment, the walls were nearly an inch (2.5cm) thick. Since outside perches might encourage predators, he did not provide them. Each species of bird had different requirements for the boxes, including the size, the height above ground, the distance between boxes, and the direction that the entrance hole faced, such as toward an open field or toward water.

There were other requirements, too. A sloped roof would prevent rainwater or snow from collecting. Young birds have weak feet, so James made boxes with rough or grooved interior walls that gave baby birds footholds when they climbed out. He supplied a recessed floor so that insects would fall through away from young birds. In addition, drainage and ventilation holes gave him easy access for monitoring and cleaning.

James's father helped him plan and build the nest boxes. "When James needed my assistance, he let me know, as frequently as he felt necessary to ensure a timely, positive response,"[9] James Sr. recalls. He taught James how to use electric tools, wear safety glasses, and clean up after cutting the wood.

On a frosty day in February 2003, James put up the boxes with assistance from Staten Island Parks Department workers. They placed four bluebird boxes along the trail. The American kestrel nest box was installed

Young Heroes: Andrew Quadrino

atop a tall pole in a densely weeded area. The barn owl box was located in a tree at the top of a hill. James selected locations near the edge of a pond for the wood duck boxes. Once the boxes were installed, the most important question remained: Would the birds use them? The only way to tell would be to check the boxes regularly.

One of James's nesting boxes hangs in a tree, ready for use.

Problems and Solutions

James had to be extremely patient when he began to monitor the nest boxes, and he still uses the same careful procedure. He explains, "I met my mom at home right after school, grabbed my binoculars, waders, screwdriver, pen, and my pad. It takes one hour to monitor the boxes. Each bird box has a number and a letter . . . so when I write any information about that box I use those identifications."[10]

James took pictures of each box and wrote his observations. One day he opened the bluebird box and saw some feathers inside. Not long after, two birds were flying near the box. James recalls, "It was an amazing feeling. When we first found eggs in a nest my mom and I wanted to jump and scream out loud."[11]

Some species of birds are distressed by intruders, while others are not. James often uses binoculars to observe American kestrels and barn owls so he can keep his distance. He has to wait for the parents to leave before he can check the nests, because the adults might attack him with their sharp beaks and claws.

The wood duck is shy and does not like to be disturbed, but the monitoring process is very important and must be done for several reasons. Harsh weather and predators are not the only dangers to the birds. Another is **invasive species**, non-native birds that take over the habitat of native species. Starlings, for example, lay their eggs in other birds' nests. When they hatch, baby starlings can take over a nest and even kill other hatchlings.

At one point James discovered that a wood duck box had four starling eggs in it. He explains: "Because I monitor the box every day, those eggs did not have a chance to become adults. I did not like that experience because the rules are that the eggs must be **exterminated**."[12] To protect his native birds, James had to remove and destroy the starling eggs.

Monitoring Progress

After the first season, James added two more bluebird boxes in another area. Today he protects additional cavity-nesting species, including the screech owl, Carolina wren, and tufted titmouse. He has also added the black-capped chickadee, purple martin, great horned owl, saw whet owl, and tree swallow to his list.

Each of the added species has different habits and behavior. Tree swallows are among the easiest for James to monitor. "Tree swallows are very mellow,"[13] he explains. He says the parents do not get upset when he inspects the boxes and the eggs or hatchlings inside. Still, they stay very close, flying overhead or sitting on a line.

James begins his monitoring by alerting the birds to his presence. He says, "I always make sure that I talk or clap before opening the box, so the birds know that I am there."[14] He holds each chick in his hands, gives it a name, and talks to it. James gently checks the bird's wings and feet and observes its behavior for any sign of problems such as bloodsucking insect **larvae** that

A member of the park service helps James hang a nesting box.

An eastern bluebird stays alert at a bird feeder. Bluebirds were the first birds James saw using the nesting boxes.

could leave the bird poorly nourished. He can tell whether a young bird is eating or not from how it looks and feels. Some signs that indicate a sick bird may be a bloated belly or inactivity. If a bird is not eating, James keeps a close eye on it, trying to diagnose the problem and come up with a solution. Once he is finished with the inspection, he records his observations. Careful monitoring gives the baby birds their best chance for survival.

Chapter Three

Success in the Field

With patience and determination, James has carefully nurtured dozens of bird families near his home. The nest boxes that he designed and built are still helping to restore threatened communities of cavity-nesting birds on Staten Island. Yet the value of his work reaches beyond the grasslands and woodlands of Mount Loretto.

James sends the data he collects to the Cornell Laboratory of Ornithology. The mission of the laboratory is to gather information about birds and other animals. The long-term goal is to preserve the **biodiversity** of earth. According to the lab's Web site, the scientists there "believe that bird enthusiasts of all ages can and do make a difference."[15] James sets an example of what a young person can accomplish.

In particular, James contributes to a project called the Birdhouse Network by serving as its ambassador. People who join the network learn to build birdhouses or nest boxes for their own neighborhoods. They gather information about the birds that use the boxes, the nests, and any eggs that result. They then send the information to scientists at Cornell. The information becomes part of a national database.

James's job as ambassador for the Birdhouse Network is to teach the public about birds and their habitats. To do this, he holds meetings to provide information about cavity-nesting birds. He hands out printed materials that tell about the birds and give tips on how to build and monitor nest boxes. He also explains the benefits of the Birdhouse Network and other Cornell projects. One such project is the Great Backyard Bird

A member of the Birdhouse Network completes work on a bird house.

Count. Each year for four days in midwinter, volunteers identify and count birds they see in their own neighborhoods. Counts are submitted through an online checklist. Scientists can use the information to learn more about bird habits and populations.

Another important part of James's job is to educate children about cavity-nesting birds. At schools and park centers, he speaks for about 45 minutes at a time and then answers questions. He has found that young children are usually curious about the eggs, what sort of food the birds eat, and how the wild birds react when James touches them. He hopes his work will help children develop a lifelong interest in birds.

James does not mind speaking in public. If he feels nervous he reminds himself that talking to a group is not a lot different from talking to people individually. The important thing is helping people learn about the birds and understand what can be done to protect them.

The President's Environmental Youth Award

James knows that every presentation is important, but he feels that the one he made in 2004 for the Environmental Protection Agency (EPA) in Washington, D.C., had a critical impact. His audience included many powerful people with the authority to make and enforce laws that protect the environment. James realized that he had a special opportunity to make people aware of the dangers the birds faced and to explain to his listeners how they could help save them.

James explains his nesting box project at a presentation for The Environmental Protection Agency (EPA) in Washington, D.C.

In 2003, after seeing one of his presentations, a school aide told James about the President's Environmental Youth Award (PEYA). The EPA created PEYA in 1971 to encourage children to become involved in protecting the environment. Each year, the president of the United States recognizes young Americans for their outstanding environmental projects. James decided to apply for the award. If he won, he could gain attention and support for his valuable work.

His project certainly met the requirements. For example, his work has had a positive impact on the local community and society. It will also have a long-term benefit for the people of Staten Island. The bird populations that James has helped are important parts of the island's ecosystems because they help keep insect and rodent populations under control. James filled out the forms, sent them off, then turned his attention to other things.

The following February, he received a telephone call from the EPA. "My mother actually received the phone call when I was not home and informed me of my win," James says. "I was going to play in a soccer game. After the news, I couldn't concentrate on the game."[16]

James's friends and family were extremely proud of him. "One of James's strongest traits is his determination, willpower, and ability to carry a plan from 'idea' to 'finish,'" says his father. "If I tell James that something can't be done, he is not discouraged and will try even harder to put his idea into action. I think that his never-say-never approach was one of the biggest factors in the success of his project."[17]

At the White House

James was honored in a ceremony in the White House East Wing on April 22, 2004. The Marine Corps Band played as the young winners from each of ten regions across the United States arrived. When everyone was seated, President George W. Bush entered the room. He gave a speech on the importance of the work the award winners had done, calling them fine young **stewards** of the environment.

Young Heroes: Andrew Quadrino

President George W. Bush congratulates James Quadrino at a White House ceremony in 2004.

"Showing concern for the environment is one way of showing your love for America," he said. "Americans are fortunate to be able to breathe clean air and enjoy the beautiful diverse landscapes of our vast continent. By getting your hands dirty and helping to clean up your communities you're putting your ideals into action and you're making America a better place."[18]

EPA administrator Steven Johnson introduced James to the audience and described his work with the birds. Bush then asked James to come forward, shook his hand, and hugged him. James had a few minutes to explain the nature of his project.

He gave a brief overview, detailing how the nest boxes contribute to the survival of cavity-nesters on Staten Island. Afterward, the president encouraged James to continue his important effort. New York senator Hillary Clinton also took time to discuss the project with James. He described the details to her and

Hillary Clinton, U.S. senator from New York, posed with James Quadrino after he received his award.

explained how she and other senators could help promote environmentalism.

When news reporters later asked for an interview, James never forgot that he was there to make people aware of the plight of the birds. He felt that the opportunity to speak at the White House had helped him to gain support for his cause. Many lawmakers realized that the survival of cavity-nesting birds depends on their having safe nesting sites undisturbed by development.

A Special Thanks

James appreciated the opportunity to speak in Washington, D.C., and is grateful for the support he has re-

James proudly accepts the 2004 President's Environmental Youth Award for his nesting box project.

ceived from his teachers, friends, and family. They have helped him and encouraged him to reach his goals. His mother says, "I learned at an early age that preservation and education are fundamental to save nature. I appreciate and will always motivate James's care and love for nature and animals. As he gets involved with the environment, he at the same time is preparing a better world and learning how to be responsible. I am proud of him for his knowledge and his desire to preserve life in any form."[19]

Chapter Four

The Work Continues

James plans to expand his project and place additional nest boxes in other parks on Staten Island. He hopes to learn more about bird biology so that he can contribute to research on avian diseases such as house finch eye disease and West Nile virus. He feels the more he understands about biodiversity, the more he can do to help the birds.

A New Project

Besides working to help birds, James has designed a project to save an endangered tree species, the American chestnut. This beautiful tree was once widespread in eastern woodlands. It was a source of food for animals ranging from birds to bears. Farmers fed the nuts to their livestock. The wood was used for everything from fence posts to furniture. In the early 1900s, however, a disease called chestnut blight killed millions of the trees. By 1950 the trees had been wiped out on the eastern coast of the

A scientist tests an American chestnut tree for disease resistance.

United States. Then, in 1981, scientists started a program to breed a chestnut tree that can resist the disease. James's project is designed to help restore the trees to **sustainable** levels.

He calls the project *Fidelis Silva*, which means "faithful forest" in Latin. He chose it because chestnuts were an important part of American history. James's plan is to involve the local community in reestablishing a healthy population of trees. He grows chestnut saplings in his backyard and distributes them to parks and responsible families.

James tracks the development of each adopted tree and keeps records of its growth. He says that getting the community involved is the best way to preserve the trees. He believes that people working together produce results well beyond the capabilities of one person working alone. In the end the trees, wildlife, and community each benefit. The trees are reintroduced into forests, thus providing food and shelter for wildlife. The community benefits because a healthy forest gives people the opportunity to enjoy the beauty of nature.

Caring for the Environment

Bird conservation will always be one of his favorite topics, but James wants to learn about other animals and habitats as well. In the future he plans to attend college to become a conservation biologist, **evolutionary biologist,** or chemist. He believes that the planet's biodiversity is facing a crisis and a good education will enable him to help fight it. One example of biodiversity in trouble is Shawangunk Ridge, in New York

State. There are plans to open a portion of the area to housing development. Although this will not threaten the entire ridge, it will break up the habitat, which will lead to a decrease in biodiversity throughout the area. James hopes to someday play a part in solving such is-

James grew American chestnut tree seedlings like these in his backyard to help restore habitat for endangered species.

Once this American chestnut seedling is replanted and fully grown it will provide food and shelter for wildlife.

sues. He says, "In the grand scheme of things, we depend on other species as they depend on us. Other species are vital for our survival."[20]

James's accomplishments illustrate that no one is too young to help protect nature. He says children can and should care about the environment because the world is theirs. In most communities there are likely to be environmental issues that need to be tackled. James's advice to others is to start small and lead by example. He says, "You must act locally before you can act globally, and if you begin to try and conserve the environment, others will follow suit."[21] An example of starting small is writing a letter to a government representative expressing concern or support for an environmental issue, such as protecting an endangered species. Another way to help would be to spend a weekend cleaning up trash in a park or on a beach. Success with small projects like these can lead to bigger ones.

Restoring Natural Habitat

One example of a larger project is restoring a local habitat to its natural state. Such a habitat provides food and shelter for the animals that live there. In a healthy pond or stream, for instance, the water is clean and free of trash. It typically supports a population of native plants that serve as food for native wildlife.

The loss of healthy habitats is the main reason species become threatened or extinct. Often, habitat loss is caused by human activity. For example, if a waterway is used for recreation, swimmers can stir up sand or mud in the water or harm wildlife. Plants may be trampled, and visitors can leave trash behind.

A young person who wants to start a campaign to preserve all or part of an area in its natural state can begin by doing research. Information about wildlife and habitats is available in newspapers, at the library, or on the Internet. These sources may list local action groups that can help.

Research can also turn up any regulations that could affect the project. For example, if the site is on private property, the owner must give permission before any action can be taken. If the site is on government property, a permit may be required. That may involve writing letters to local government officials explaining the idea and outlining the benefits.

If money is needed to help pay for the project, a young environmentalist can organize fundraising events

Young Heroes: Andrew Quadrino

such as garage sales, bake sales, or car washes. Once the project begins, removing litter and trash is frequently the first step in restoring an ailing habitat. If the habitat is a waterway, another important activity is to identify and remove invasive species of plants. These are nonnative plants that can take over local ecosys-

Young volunteers pose for a photo after picking up trash along a river in Los Angeles, CA.

tems, crowding out the natives. Such plants can be useless or even harmful to native animals.

A Nature-Friendly Backyard

Restoring a habitat is a big job. For young people who prefer a smaller project, a perfect opportunity to help the environment is as near as a backyard. A large space is not required to create a butterfly garden that offers food and shelter for migrating butterflies such as the monarch. During spring and fall migration, monarchs travel hundreds of miles or more. Along the way they rely on a supply of plants, particularly milkweed, for food and a place to lay their eggs. Such nectar-rich plants grow easily in small gardens or in pots on a porch, patio, or rooftop. They can be a lifesaver for the butterflies. The inexpensive seeds can be purchased in garden shops or ordered on the Internet.

Another way to help the environment is to create a rain garden. Rainwater runoff from roofs and driveways erodes soil and may carry motor oil and other pollutants to waterways. A garden designed to catch and

Children study the creatures that live in their school garden.

filter the runoff is a healthy solution. All that is needed is a clear area at the edge of a downspout, driveway, or other paved surface where rainwater can soak into the soil. The garden works best if it is dug out so that the base is about six inches (15cm) below the surface, then filled with soft soil and plants. The plants that work best will depend on the climate, but local wildflowers, grasses, and ferns are excellent choices. A rain garden conserves water, prevents erosion, reduces water pollution, and can provide a habitat for wildlife.

Children concerned about nature can find a way to help, no matter how minor or how serious the problem. In the words of United Nations secretary-general Kofi Annan, "The preservation of biodiversity is not just a job for governments . . . each and every individual has a role to play."[22]

Notes

Chapter 1: The Boy Who Saves Birds
1. E-mail interview with the author, February 27, 2006.
2. E-mail interview with the author, February 15, 2006.
3. E-mail interview with the author, February 27.
4. E-mail interview with the author, February 15.
5. E-mail interview with the author, February 15.
6. E-mail interview with the author, February 15.
7. E-mail interview with the author, February 27.

Chapter 2: Problems and Solutions
8. E-mail interview with the author, February 27.
9. E-mail interview with the author, February 27.
10. E-mail interview with the author, February 27.
11. E-mail interview with the author, February 27.
12. E-mail interview with the author, February 27.
13. E-mail interview with the author, February 27.
14. E-mail interview with the author, February 27.

Chapter 3: Success in the Field
15. The Cornell Laboratory of Ornithology Web site, http://www.birds.cornell.edu.
16. E-mail interview with the author, February 15.
17. E-mail interview with the author, February 15.
18. "President Bush Presents Environmental

Youth Awards," speech given April 22, 2004. www.whitehouse.gov/news/releases/2004/04/20040422-7.html.
19. E-mail interview with the author, February 27.

Chapter 4: The Work Continues
20. E-mail interview with the author, February 27.
21. E-mail interview with the author, February 27.
22. Kofi Annan, "Message on the International Day for Biological Diversity," May 22, 2003. www.biodiv.org/doc/press/2003/pr-2003-05-22-bioday-un-en.pdf.

Glossary

alpacas: Long-haired llama-like mammals native to South America.

avian: Relating to birds.

biodiversity: The range of different kinds of living things within ecosystems.

ecosystem: A group of interdependent organisms and their environment.

evolutionary biologist: A scientist who studies the development of species.

exterminated: Killed or destroyed.

insatiable: Impossible to satisfy.

invasive species: A nonnative species that takes over the habitat of a native species.

larvae: The immature form of insects.

ornithology: The scientific study of birds.

predators: Animals that hunt, kill, and eat other animals.

species: A group of animals that have shared traits and that are able to interbreed.

stewards: Caretakers or managers of resources.

sustainable: Able to keep balance of resources that allows them to be used without being used up.

For Further Exploration

Books

Sneed B. Collard, *Acting for Nature: What Young People Around the World Are Doing to Protect the Environment*. Berkeley, CA: Heyday Books, 2000. This is a collection of biographies of young people who have organized projects to save the environment.

Rhonda Lucas Donald, *Water Pollution*. Chicago: Children's Press, 2002. This book provides a simple overview of water, wetlands, and water pollution, as well as suggestions for cleaning up pollution.

Suzanne J. Murdico, *Volunteering to Help the Environment*. Chicago: Children's Press, 2000. This book details what children can do to make a difference for the environment.

Christine Peterson, *Conservation*. Chicago: Children's Press, 2004. An introduction to life science and conservation, this book includes information on environments and how they may be changed by humans.

Linda Schwartz, *Earth Book for Kids: Activities to Help Heal the Environment*. Santa Barbara: The Learning Works, 1990. This activity book on how to care for the earth defines environmental terms and concepts.

Web Sites

All About Birds (www.birds.cornell.edu). This Cornell Laboratory of Ornithology interactive site enables young people to be part of wildlife data collection. It includes Project Feeder Watch, the Great Backyard Bird Count, and a selection of nest box cams.

Children of the Earth United (www.childrenoftheearth. org). This is a site where kids can learn about the environment and share their ideas. It covers a wide range of environmental topics, including great books, ecocareers, nature programs, native wisdom, and amazing animals.

Environmental Kids Club (www.epa.gov/kids). This site is maintained by the EPA. It offers tips about how to help to protect the air, water, and land. It also offers games, pictures, and stories.

The Green Squad (www.nrdc.org/greensquad). This Natural Resources Defense Council site shows how to help schools become more environment-friendly. It includes fact sheets on energy, water, asthma, air pollution, and other topics. In an interactive program, kids move from room to room in school learning how to make ecofriendly changes.

Kids F.A.C.E. (Kids For A Clean Environment) (www.kids face.org). This Web site gives information on environmental issues and action for children. It also explains how children can start a chapter of Kids F.A.C.E.

Monarch Waystation Program (www.monarchwatch.org/ws/index.html). This is the Monarch Watch site of the Kansas Biological Survey of the University of Kansas. It gives information about monarch butterflies, explains how to create a monarch waystation to help migrating butterflies, tells how to order a waystation seed kit, and how to certify a waystation.

Tree of Life Project (http://tolweb.org/tree/learn). This is the kids' page on the Tree of Life Web Project Web site, a collaborative effort of biologists from around the world. It includes games and projects that help children learn about local environments.

Index

activism
 community involvement, 32
 environmental projects, 34–37, 39
American chestnut tree, 30, 32
American kestrels, 15–16, 17
animals, 6–8
Annan, Kofi, 39

barn owls, 16, 17
beech trees, 12
biodiversity
 crisis, 32–33
 importance, 34
 preservation, 21
 role of individual, 39
Birdhouse Network, 21–22
birds
 attracting different species, 13–15
 education and, 22–23
 importance of, 11
 invasive species, 17–18
 sick, 18, 20
bluebird boxes, 15, 17, 18
Brazil, 7–8
Bush, George W., 25–27
butterfly gardens, 37

camping trips, 6
Carolina wrens, 18
cavity-nesting birds, 13, 18
 see also specific species
chestnut blight, 30, 32
Clinton, Hillary, 27
community involvement, 32
Cornell University Laboratory of Ornithology, 11, 21, 22–23

ecosystem balance, 9, 11, 32
Environmental Protection Agency (EPA), 23–27

Fidelis Silva (Faithful Forest) project, 30, 32
fire, 11
fundraising, 35–36

Great Backyard Bird Count, 22–23

habitats
 destruction of, 8–9, 11, 32–33
 gardens as, 37, 39
 restoration of, 35–37

insects
 controlling, 11
 larvae, 18, 20
invasive species
 birds, 17–18
 plants, 36–37

Jeopardy (television program), 6
Johnson, Steven, 27

land developers, 8–9, 32–33

monarch butterflies, 37
Monsignor Farrell High School, 6
Mount Loretto Unique Area, 8, 11, 12–14

Mythbusters (television program), 6

Index

nature preserves, 8, 11, 12–14
nest boxes
   Birdhouse Network and, 21–22
   importance, 11
   installing, 15–16
   monitoring, 17–18, 20
   requirements, 14–15
   sites, 12–14
New York State Department of Environment Conservancy (DEC), 12

plants
   invasive species, 36–37
   rain garden, 39
predators, 17
President's Environmental Youth Award (PEYA), 4, 24–28
public speaking, 23, 24, 27, 28

Quadrino, James, Sr. (father), 6, 15, 25
Quadrino, James Andrew, 4–6
   awards, 24–28
   on becoming an activist, 34
   on biodiversity, 34
   characteristics of, 25
   on choosing birds to provide boxes for, 14
   on fire at Mount Loretto, 11
   future plans, 32
   on interest in animals, 7–8
   on monitoring boxes, 17, 18
   on volunteering at zoo, 8
   on winning President's Environmental Youth Award, 25
Quadrino, John (brother), 4, 5
Quadrino, Joseph (brother), 4, 5
Quadrino, Maria (mother), 5, 6, 29

Quammen, David, 6

rain gardens, 37, 39
Rawls, Wilson, 6
reading, 6
robotics, 6
rodent control, 11
Ronaldo (dog), 6

screech owls, 18
Shawangunk Ridge, New York, 32–34
soccer, 6
Song of the Dodo (Quammen), 6
sports, 6
starlings, 18
Staten Island (New York City)
   Parks Department workers, 15–16
   wildlife areas, 8, 11
   Zoo, 8

Terry (dog), 6
toucans, 7–8
trees
   endangered species, 30, 32
   variety in Mount Loretto, 12–13
tree swallows, 18
tufted titmice, 18
turtles, 7

Verdinho (canary), 6

weather, 15, 17
Where the Red Fern Grows (Rawls), 6
wood ducks, 16, 17
wrestling, 6

Picture Credits

Cover, Courtesy of James A. Quadrino
© Peter Arnold/Alamy, 9
Associated Press, AP, 26
© Gary Braasch/CORBIS, 31
© Gary W. Carter/CORBIS, 20
© Martin Jones/CORBIS, 38
© Royalty free/CORBIS, 22
© Joseph Sohm/ChromoSohm, Inc., 36
Courtesy of James A. Quadrino, 5, 7, 10, 13, 14, 16, 19, 24, 27, 28, 33, 34

About the Author

Q.L. Pearce has written more than one hundred trade books for children and more than thirty classroom workbooks and teacher manuals on the topics of reading, science, math, and values. Pearce has written science-related articles for magazines; regularly gives presentations at schools, bookstores, and libraries; and is a frequent contributor to the educational program of the Los Angeles County Fair. She is the assistant regional adviser for the Society of Children's Book Writers and Illustrators in Orange, San Bernardino, and Riverside counties in California and is a member of the advisory board for California State University–Fullerton's Writing for Children program.

Maywood Public Library
459 Maywood Avenue
Maywood, NJ 07607

JB
QUADRINO

5/07

Maywood Public Library
Maywood, NJ 07607